NATHANIEL.S.BIRD

◆ ◆ ◆

NO END TO WRITING

◆ ◆ ◆

Nathaniel .s. Bird

Books available in e.books also paperback by
Nathaniel S Bird.

book 1-The beautiful colours of life
book 2-The human challenging games
book 3-Troubles on every bend and corners
book 4-Actions speaks for itself
book 5-Ghetto living
book 6-You can get there if you try
book 7-You don't even know who I am
book 8-You think you know it all
book 9-The battle for cash
book 10-Our world is filled with wonders
book 11-It's not over until it's over
book 12-The race has to be run
book 13 -Those who are determined will succeed
book 14-The waiting game is not easy
book 15-The foolishness of folly
book 16-Don't lose focus
book 17-Around and around our world does spin
book 18-Treasure hunt
book 19 -Chocolate Dread and Blue Shoes
book 20-Money makes the world go around.
book 21-The light shines brighter on the other side
book 22-The journey of life
book 23-The days of my life
book 24-Just a dream
book 25-Every body
book 26- time clock
book 27-secret mysterious friend
book 28-Birdy the black guy from Port Talbot,South
Wales(book one).
book 29-Birdy the black guy from Port Talbot,South

Wales(book two).
book 30-Birdy the black guy from Port Talbot South Wales(book 3).

❖ ❖ ❖

NO END TO WRITING
Where are the **WORDS** of wisdom coming **FROM**
they must be **FLOATING** in **THE AIR**
words very **PRECIOUS EXCELLENT**
words which are fine also very **FAIR.**
The words of wisdom
were **HERE** in **TIMES BEGINNING**
they shall be here **ON EARTH**
in **THE END** of **TIME**
although the **HEAVEN'S** and the earth
may **PASS AWAY**
wisdom will **STILL** be here
DELIGHTFUL in it's **PLAY.**
Time it is **ENDLESS**
so to the words of wisdom as well
the words of **OUR MOUTHS**
they are very **POWERFULL**
words do **SHOW** and **TELL.**
If you **RESPECT** the word
it shall teach you
MAKING you **BECOME CLEVER**
EDUCATED even **WISE.**
THERE IS NO END to **WRITING**
go to **THE LIBRARY**
then you will **SEE** for **YOURSELVES**
BOOK upon books
LOOK how **WELL PACKED** are the **SHELVES.**

it goes to **SHOW PEOPLE**
they **LOVE READING** books
whether **FICTION** or **NON FICTION**
it seem **LIKE** any type of book
as **LONG** as it's **INTERESTING**
ENTERTAINING to them
it certainly is **WORTH** the **LOOK** .
SPEND A **LITTLE MONEY**
go out and **BUY** yourself a book
it is **SOMETHING YOU** do not **THROW AWAY**
even when you **HAVE** finished
READING to it's **END**
if you **DO NOT** hold onto it
you **WILL PROBABLY HAND** it
to **ONE** of your good **FRIEND'S**
who will **MORE** than likely **READ** it
then keep it or hand it on once again.

◆ ◆ ◆

INDEX

NO.1   WORDS

A single letter right next to one another
can create a single word
a word can be made up of even just a single letter
if this letter is a vowel.
    A word can be short
    it can also be long
    when we join words to words
    we can create a lovely song.
Words constantly joined together fluently
created speech with langauge's
so we can communicate together
her him you also me.
    The human race they are very fortunate
    for with them exist real word's
    which teaches us all daily
    while we live in this wide busy world.
If you have respect for word's
they can lift you up
placing you in a respectable position very high
you could be seated high in office
governing the whole of mankind.

NO.2   FROM

From our young early tender times
when we were just born being only a few month's old
we constantly relied on our parent's
cuddled up in their arms in our homely home's.
    We couldn,t speak we couldn,t talk
    we could not say a single word
    the only sound with noise we made
    was crying so we could be noticed even be heard.
It was our form of communication
this was the only way we knew how to react
when we needed some attention
we would loudly cry we would not relax.
    When we were hungry needing feeding
    even when our nappies were soaking wet
    it was that time for communication once again
    we would not give up on our crying
    until mum came sorted us out then finally left.

◆ ◆ ◆

NO.3   FLOATING

The word's we can not see
as we start to speak
when we open up our mouths

we can only hear this is certain without a doubt.
    Why can't we not see the word's ?
    when we talk or when we shout
    it's because the word's we speak are invisible
    as we are starting to speak out.
Why are words invisible ?
please tell me why is it word's we just can't see ?
well the floating words they are a vapour
which is just air it is spirit
shared between you even me.
    What is a spirit a spirit ?
    is something which is real
    it doesn,t have a body form
    it drifts it float
    it also lives on and on and on and on.

◆ ◆ ◆

NO.4   THE AIR

All around us invisible wise word's
are floating in the air
the air which is the breath of life
you had better be aware.
    The air covers the whole of planet earth
    the whole world's atmosphere
    keeping us all alive
    it is very precious it is very rare.
The words of wisdom
they are floating through the air
expensive are the words
try capturing some of them if you dare.

If you are lucky and fortunate
to catch a tiny little bit
you had better now be prepared also ready
for wisdom is now going to take you
on life's wise amazing trip.

◆ ◆ ◆

NO.5   PRECIOUS

Very precious are the word's of wisdom
which are given to women and men
it is handed down to the nations of the world
for us all to learn to speak and to even understand.
   It teaches every one of us
   all the things we need to know about our planet
   it teaches those who seek for it
   the things they may need to know
   so they in time may greatly benefit.
Wisdom is very benificial
to all those who are wise in heart
it will cut corners in this life for you
if you embrace and nuture it
it will refined you making you become more sharp.
   It will build up a great character inside of you
   it will open wide your living eye's
   it will protect you it will cherish you
   it's because wisdom when it called out
   you did not ignore neither did you deny.

◆ ◆ ◆

NO.6   EXCELLENT

Didn,t you know the value of wisdom is excellent
didn,t you know the word's of wisdom are high rated
it is in the class of excellence
so why should you dis-respect it.
   Why abuse the words you speak
    by forming with your lips also mouth
    in-expensive word's very cheap.
All the wise people love knowledge
inside of knowledge it is wise words they will find
words of uprightness
filled with rhythm's poetrys and rhyme's.
   Hidden secrets it will reveal to you
   wisdom it will turn your minds wise
   for wisely seeking searching for it
   you will soon realise you have stumbled upon
   a real life winning prize.

◆ ◆ ◆

NO.7   FAIR

This is how fair and wise word's are
they pick select then choose
refining those hearts with minds

they desire to dwell in
high rated word's are not for fools.
   Word's of a very low value
      grammar which just ain,t worth the while
      invest themselves in the minds with hearts
      of all those people who love to live very vile.
You can not fool about with word's
you will realise in the end
you are just fooling your ownself
the word you didn't take serious
it is very serious and doesn't pretend.
      Don,t turn honesty into lies
      if you do then your word's are going to let you down
      because you are trying to turn
      something real into falsehood
      it,s you in time who is going to be resembling
      the foolish clown.

◆ ◆ ◆

NO.8   HERE

The word's of wisdom
has been here before times beginning
long before this planet earth was established
before it was properly formed
it was here before the existance
of the evening dusk with the morning dawn.
   It has been here since everlasting time commenced
   even though everlasting has no beginning
   right infront of everlasting
   wisdom would always joyfully dance rejoice and sing.

It is wisdom who handed out
all the planets in outer space their names
all the host of heavenly stars it has totalled in number's
given names.
    Eternal is the word
    it is without beginning and end
    invincible undistructable untouchable
    my reading friend.

◆ ◆ ◆

NO.9   TIMES

Time as been moving throughout the ages
the human population has increased
nations have grown bigger
warring wars though as not ceased.
    Civilization is more civilized
    though many wars still do exist
    helping aids is sent to many nation's
    who are on the verge of starvation very near to perish.
There is always room for more improvement's
humanity though does try it's best
while we are alive and living
among these challenging times
the *earthly worldly real contest.*
    As time moves along throughout the ages
    it experiences many different periods
    moments with stages
    no wars cover the lands the planet dwells in peace
    there is not a single war violently furiously
    wildly roaring while raging

a generation of equity justice fairness with peace.
Righteous noblemen ruling
in whole integrity from the very top
the poor with the needy are well looked after
injustice is now for a time
placed on cease temporally stopped.
   The people of the lands are all happy
    for everyone is dwelling in peace
    locked up nice and securily
    is the nature of the demonic spiritual earthly beast.

◆ ◆ ◆

NO.10   BEGINNING

We start learning from the beginning
right from the very start
as soon as the power of the spirit of the word
enters deep into our young brandnew beating hearts.
   We are learn from very early in life
    watching while secretively learning from our parents
    the mind taking in informations
    towards our direction knowledge is being sent.
Very active are the young minds of children
very thirsty and eager
wanting to take so much information in
as soon as they wake up arising early in the morning
their learning time in life again
straight away starts to begin.
   Little young souls filled up with curiosity
    always willing desiring really needing to get to know
    very early in this life searching seeking trying to find

for they to inwardly with knowledge wish to grow.

◆ ◆ ◆

NO.11   EARTH

The earth is established forever
surrounded by great ocean's with blue moving sea's
small hills with high mountain's
desert lands trillion's of tall wooden trees.
  Cliffs with dangerous deadly deep drops
   waterfalls,running streams,water springs
   green pastures,fields filled with vegetations
   diverse crops wheat grains barley
   the land is alive with colourful flowers it seems to sing.
Contenants very large in size
covered with different countries
filled with parishes districts,boroughs,county's,cities
towns,villages inhabited by people
not left desolate empty with no one living in.
   People of all nationalities
   all belonging to different family kinds
   speaking foreign langauges
    to separate divide define.
The earth which is very large in size
stretches itself for thousands and thousands of miles
filled to the brim of living species
creatures of all types many are versitile.

◆ ◆ ◆

NO.12   THE END

Mostly everything has and end
but with the word's of wisdom
there is no end to them at all
for wisdom is spiritually eternal
created to stand up great also fantastically tall
never ever to fail neither fall.
   There is an end to every human life
   animals birds reptiles fishes in the seas
   insects with every other living species
   even the ever green growing trees.
The sun with moon may one day
lose their splendid shine
while all the twinkling stars
drop out from the heavenly night sky.
   The high tall rugged cliffs
   crumble collapse and fall
   as the great mountains tumble
   crumbling into the oceans with seas.
Wisdom though will still be fully preserved
while it still delightfully shines forth positively alive
in it's unique splendid splendours of holiness
it's true real living beautiful colours of brilliant beauties
it will continue to shine forever brightly fine.

◆ ◆ ◆

NO.13　TIME

You can not attach time to the word's of wisdom
for it is in an entirely different class
one day time may run out
the word's of wisdom are around forever
throughout eternity to last.
  Time is very precious
  the words of wisdom is the most precious of them all
  you had better listen out for it's soft silent calling voice
  when to you it starts to wisely call.
Listen to the wise people
they will show and they will teach
it is the word which has made them wise with wisdom
see how they all now walk confidently on their feets.
  Their minds are not lacking
  for the knowledge of life they have bought
  intellectual intelligence real wisdom
  this is the process of their thinking thoughts.
They store up knowledge all of the time
which shall not be unused wasting away
it will always come in very useful to them
sometime in thier lives along moving times pathways.

◆　◆　◆

NO.14   HEAVEN

The word's of wisdom they come from heaven
there is where it abodes also dwells
it starts getting polluted
when it descends down to earth
because of all of earths perverse spells.
  Downgraded it becomes
   corrupted by the mouths of women and men
  even ill spoken of by the little naughty children.
In heaven it stays whole and pure
inspiring all the angels
who dwell in the perfection of peace
it is there wisdom increase more in strenght and power
it's amazing energies will never cease.
   All mysterious mystical marvels
   dwell inside of wisdom safely
   it is filled up with heavenly secrets
   for very descrete are the ways of wisdom you will see.

◆ ◆ ◆

NO.15   PASS WAY

Even though the heavens and earth may pass away
the word's of wisdom is here forever to stay
moving itself from generation to generation

showing us while telling us all information's
about the forgotten passed days.
   Great men with women showing us all
   important events which happened in their days
   era,s moments with interesting times
   writing them down all inside of books also onto scripts
   so we may be able to find out
   reading about them in these future times.
The olden days may have passed away
it's time though have been re-captured
by all those people who were wise
recording their times of living days
which to them were filled up with many a surprise.
      They have handed us all a favour
       by remembering that one day
      our time will start and finally arrive
      making all in our days to know
      many a thing takes place beneath our heavenly skies.

◆ ◆ ◆

NO.16   STILL

A world without word's
would be like everything is standing still
for although there would be people walking all around
the atmosphere it would be very chilled
   No one calling out,no voices to be heard
   a world of quietness very weird silence
   to myself I would be finding all things very bizzare
   it would be very obsurd.
Our mouths would hardly be moving

most of the time it would be motionless and still
the only time it would be actively busy
would be when we are hungry needing eating.
   No voices singing sweet lovely songs
    no vocal chords are working in our throats
     no sweet melodies early in the mornings dawn
    arguements contentions bickering
     would not now exist but would of been long ago gone.
No-one would be in a position
to show educate neither teach
for words where never created
to keep us standing confidently on our learning feets.

◆ ◆ ◆

NO.17 DELIGHTFUL

Wisdom in its lowest purest form
it is filled with might and delight
all the simplest form of good word's
would appear into our minds
in the days also throughout the nights.
    If a person was filled with wisdom
     their face would shine very fine
     they would be filled to the brim
     of wonderful joy inside their hearts
     delightfully loving enjoying life,s natural
     remedies rythmns.
Excellent would be their speech
the whole entire world they would be glad to teach
the wonders of lifes extremely interesting facts
for they know the real wisdom they do not lack.

Along the pathways of earthly worldly life
they delight themselves daily
 along it's marvellous ways
 guided by the powerful forces of wisdom
 which secretively inwardly teaches showing them
 how not in his life to totally go astray.

◆ ◆ ◆

NO.18   PLAY

Don,t you know,can,t you not see even understand
it is the word which adds extra fun
to all of our daily plans
it allows us to create funny word's
which just pops up from out of our mouths
causing us to laugh while having great terrific fun
as we happily mess about.
  That simple little thing we call the word
  it play's a massive part in all of our lives
  if the words of wisdom did not exist
  it would be near to impossible for us human's to exist
  for by the beasts of the lands
  we all would eventually be eaten alive.
We all would be as dumb as the animals of the earth
surely they in time would over power us all
their physical strenght with speed
would eventually overtake us
one by one we would all bite the dust
collapse we would certainly fall.
    Our time on the land would be threatened
    for the intelligence of wisdom

as been removed from one and all.
The simple word's we speak
it does protect while sheltering us
teaching us how to create
high great concrete protective walls
so we may all dwell safely in our homes with cities
while our little tender children happily play laughing
as they joyfully shout out in gladness then loudly call.

◆ ◆ ◆

NO.19 ENDLESS

I have told you already
I will remind you once again
the word's of wisdom they are endless
forever eternal my reading friend.
   Wise are the word's of life
    for it as seen it has also been shown
   all of creation with its hidden secret's
    which have been withheld hidden from this world.
Endless secrets are stored up with wisdom
it is the bridge between this life and the there-after
all those who love wisdom love eternal life
those who hate wisdom
love death with all it's deadly disaster's.
   Delightful are the words of wisdom
    for it know's it is created to forever exist
    it has a great reason for its great joy of delightfulness
    to live its full existance in eternal bliss
Timeless ageless exceeding all limit's with bounds
the light in it's high superior position

has been given it's name
by the most excellent superior wisdom.

◆ ◆ ◆

NO.20

OUR MOUTHS

Our mouths do you realise
how bored they would be
if the word didn't exist
extra sorrows with sadness
would pile up into the hearts inside of our chest.
　We would all be walking around as mute people
　confused with ourselves
　because we don't know how to communicate
　which would cause more pains
　to our hearts made of flesh
　which is very prone to ache even more then break.
We would all be left in the dark without word's
the light in our life will no more brightly shine
disabled would all our mouths now be
for taken away from our lives is something very fine.
　No kind gracious word's no sweet loving word's
　only mumbling coughing some hick-ups with burping
　the melodies have now gone from the morning birds

you now do not hear even a single chirping.

◆ ◆ ◆

NO.21   POWERFULL

Now I am going to remind you
how powerful the word's of wisdom really are
they are deriving from a unique
divine holy sacred place
way beyond the silver moon
way passed all those glittering twinkling stars.
   It dwells with all which is with perfection
   bursting with supreme superior energies
   it,s filled with the beauty of love
   flowing with positive energies.
Wisdom it is for the wise people
for the simple minded belongs the foolishness of folly
it's the time to make that sensible decision
so your future days may not be stripped looking empty.

◆ ◆ ◆

NO.22   SHOW

The *show of life* continues on
the *real life living show*
people walking all about

upon their ten human toes.
   Looking with their eyes
   at you me and everybody
   mouths talking lips smiling
   hearts feeling joyfull and merry.
Light feets happy in dance
the hips are rocking to and fro
hands waving some clapping
the mouth with lips together
are shouting come on lets play some more.
   Feets actively busy walking all around
   your legs are activated
   while your ears are taking
   in all the worldly sounds.
The fresh air which daily circulates us
breathed in through our mouths with nose
keeping us all alive still in existance
while our eyes are constantly on the seek
on the observe.

◆ ◆ ◆

NO.23   TELL

There is so much in life to see
there are so many places to travel to also explore
our world our planet it is beaming with life
of this I do know you are fully aware
as time moves itself along on it's travel's
through the days weeks with months also years.
   There is some much ticking time tells
    while showing us

it shows all the good people of it's lands
it's tender mercies with loving cares.
Will you be fortunate to have many good stories to tell
will you be blessed
in having many true real stories to tell
when you arrive reaching those fine old years
where you are still attracted
to positivities wonderful spells.
Up there in the future days waiting for you
in those days where your children's children
are all surrounding you
those precious grand children
even great grand children too
a solid part of the young family tree
it's your dear souls minds with hearts
they all keep paying full attention to.

◆ ◆ ◆

NO.24 RESPECT

Learn to respect the word's of your mouth
for it will show all people if you are respectful
decent sensible speach your lips will then find
the word's pushed out from your tongue
will be meaningful.
Your own heart will then select
choosing your word's
as you are talking of what is right
the word's which are proper to say.
It's your own mouth with tongue
which will be trying and tasting the selected words

knowing only healthy fine words shall flow wisely
from out of your clean speaking lips today.
   Perverse dirty filthy lies
   your heart has slipped right out of gear
  it,s negativity your whole nature is now calling out too
   evil with wickedness will now draw itself more near.
Move your mouth from speaking guile
 take from off your tongue the word's of deceit
 bitter word's to the lips of the good
are very unhealthy to their heart no where near sweet.

◆ ◆ ◆

NO.25 MAKING

We do not make word's
it is the word's which makes us
creating in us our personalities with characters
forming while at the same time shaping us.
   Making us grow up into a better or worse person
    it's all up to us if we want to become a good person
    or be some one who is bad
   gracious kind word's belong to the good
   rough tough brutal violent are the words of the sad.
We are all a production the making of our ownselves
as we daily live and grow
we only reap in times future
the present things we daily sow.
   The wise learn how to perfect their moves
   as they live in life as they daily grow
   there is always time to learn from our mistakes
   while adjusting making improvement's

as the days appear then disappear then go.

◆ ◆ ◆

NO.26 BECOME

It is through the word's you are speaking
which defines making you what you are right now
or what you will soon become
a good sensible character maybe a bad one
underneath our eternal sun.
  Words can mould your way of thinking
  good word's lead onto more greater words
  negative attaches itself onto more negativity
  of this matter you had better start to observe.
Are you a born liar
who daily love telling fibs
not taking anything serious
you had better start changing the way how you live.
    You don,t care much for your future
    if you do it only concerns cash money
  everthing else come after this s or well below this
  character is of no importance in your words to give.

◆ ◆ ◆

NO.27 CLEVER

Just look how clever word's are
really they fascinate my heart mind with soul
they make note while identifying
the subject you get to know as a whole.
    Word's can create in an individual persons mind
    a very exclusive brilliant bright idea
    bringing treasures with fine riches into their lives
    allowing this person to have a fine future
    filled with blessings mingled in with happy cheers.
Respect then the word's of life
you then will be respected by the power of the word
it will lead you because through your word's of mouth
to meet up with better greater people who are dear.
    Those who dis-respect the word's of wisdom
    will be left stranded
    all those of a perverse tongue with bitter mouths
    will be left standing still
    they will be going no-where fast in the future
    because of all that vulgar foolish talking.
Be now smart please be careful
what you say also what you speak
for word's can keep you standing strong
they can also knock you from off your feet.

                ◆ ◆ ◆

NO.28   EDUCATED

You could never become educated
if it were not for the word itself
for it's the word which as educated you
for the simple fact

that you have shown respect to the very word
so in gratitude you shall receive in time some wealth.
　　You studied hard you put in good effort
　　you never stopped revising
　　you passed your tests with all examinations
　　now you are slowly seeing
　　your position in this life is rising.
People know you are not silly neither stupid
you have had your graduation's passing your degree's
for you allowed your mind to take in information
you know all the studying did not come with ease.
　It is through your respect in wanting to learn
　you are now sacrificing your worldly time in it's turn
　which is sensible not time wasting
　in the oncoming future
　you now are due to properly earn.

◆ ◆ ◆

NO.29　　　WISE

Now it,s wise word's I love also adore
word's of wisdom my ears desire
the word's can teach also sharpen
bringing inspiration's so I feel inspired.
　　Intelligent useful word's
　　for all who want to learn
　　for this kind of information
　　my mind seeks for and daily yearn's.
Word's which will benefit me
word's which will greatly enhance teaching me
showing me how to improve my living life

real true healthy wise word's
which are pure correct honest and right indeed.
   I don,t want to be looked on as the silly idiot
   neither do I want to be branded as the local fool
   no honour is found in this
   a name which is unfit
   which shall never be positioned to bare rule.

◆ ◆ ◆

NO.30   THERE IS

Didn,t you know there is a lot
in life for us to learn
little by little day by day
we all do and must take our turn.
   There is life out here in this great wide world
    true life for me and you to find
   it's a real true life I am seeking for
   I don,t intend to live this one life
   poor neither spiritually blind.
Out there in this world there are so many things
to witness seek find and also see
days weeks with months rolling towards us
all wrapped up in mysterious beauties.
   Days filled up with hidden secrets
   never empty void neither bleak
   we just need to open our spiritual eyes
   then learn to wisely seek.

◆ ◆ ◆

NO.31 NO END

Forever eternal without an ending
lasting longer than any human mind
which is created to imagine also think
out of this world above this planet
to the words of wisdom
the universe it is just another titled thing.
    The word indentifies then makes note
    gives a name with a title to everything
    a very high position it has in existance
    it is above mostly everything.
Surpassing all orbits with dimensions
for this to wisdom gives titles with names too
it's powers are infinete
wisdom stays forever loyal very true.
    It has the victory over death
    immortal are all it's splendid glorious pathways
    shinning glowing eternally forever
    never ever will it,s wise glowing lights ever fade.

◆ ◆ ◆

NO.32 WRITING

Written word's spilt out onto paper
through intelligent thoughts with imaginations

mixed with inner emotion's
experiences coming from the author's life
he would love to share amongst the nation's.
   Word's flowing through him for his heart is opened
   ready and always willing to receive
   the precious wise word's for he is a seeker of wisdom
   which in him as now awoken that special token.
Everybody has a talent
hidden deep down inside of their heart
are you wise enough to dig it up
I intend for my gift in life to perfom it,s playing part.
   It would be very unwise for me
   to waste away my given talent
   certainly this would not be smart
   it would be better I didn't recieve it at all
   than casting it away to the swines
   dogs wolves with hungry sharks.

◆ ◆ ◆

NO.33

THE LIBRARY

The word's of wisdom they are inside of our hearts
implanted into our souls with minds
we just need to learn that bit more

in how to look inside of ourselves
than looking all around in this world
left right up and down infront also behind.
　　Many who are seeking for wisdom
　　believe to themselves by reading many books
　　this will make them wise
　　it's off to the library they are now walking
　　to collect for themselves another borrowing book
　　at this very moment in time.
The fear of the Lord
this is the beginning of wisdom
simply step away from doing what is wrong
throughout the yearly seasons
these actions makes the mind mentally positive
also spiritually strong.

◆ ◆ ◆

NO.34　　　SEE

Even if you were born physically blind
if in this world you could never ever see
one thing you will not be missing out on
it is the spiritual words of life
which is for you including everybody.
　　Physical eyes are not needed
　　to be connected to the spiritual words
　　the words of wisdom are already connected to us
　　of this you best observe.
Deep down inside of your hearts they lay
right down there silently they dwell
you just need to learn how to fish them up

from out of life's real deep living precious well.
    A person of understanding
    they will be able to draw them right up
    through skill with mental ability
    it will not be because of that thing
    the simple people call pure luck.

◆ ◆ ◆

NO.35 YOURSELVES

Come on now all you people
don,t you think it's about that time
you started behaving yourselves
putting your speach in the right order
so then everyone can make sense of yourself.
    Your conduct's also this need to improve
    so then you may achieve
    finer things for yourself in this life
    while you are daily passing on through.
Remember none of us are perfect
we all have to make mistake's
so then we may gain in experience and learn
life itself is a learning teaching process
it,s all a apart of life's *real living games.*

◆ ◆ ◆

NO.36 BOOK

I do hope you find this little book interesting
I do hope it inspires bringing inspirations to your mind
books are writing for all types of reason's
some are written to educated also guide
while some are written to entertain you
all through the days afternoon
evenings with the nights.
  My books are written to inspire
  to influence to guide.
  hoping to lift up high your spirit's
  taking you on a spiritual ride
Word's written easy to understand
wellsprings of wisdom
for growing teenagers with young adults
including mature women with adult men.
   I do hope you appreciate my style of writing
   the way the words roll interact then combine
   I hope you see they are of a certain class
   which is in league with what is fine all of the while.

❖ ❖ ❖

NO.37 LOOK

Take note of all what is happening around you

watch look listen then learn
have a little ponder use your thinking minds
before you start to realise
this now in life is your given turn.
    You now presently are joined
     to this real living generation
     you living life time as finally arrived
     this is not the time for you to be acting blind
      while you are living out your moving moments
    amongst the whole of mankind.
Open wide those living eye's
at the same time do not close tight
shutting your heart's
forgetting then in this living life
you to have a real role to play an important part.
    Look now at your life,s present situations
     tell me now does it make you feel happy
     maybe it makes you feel very sad
     if you are feeling you don't feel fond of it
    then you have been dealt in life
     a bad pack of playing cards.

◆ ◆ ◆

NO.38 WELL

I can certainly say one thing which is sure
this is the words they serve us very well
it is the greatest gift our *creator* have given to us
which upon *H.I.S* earth we daily dwell .
   Good words cheer up our heart's with our spirits
    keeping us feeling mentally fine

eat now drink also keep you merry
  go now on your way
  keeping your feet on the honest line.
Life will treat all those well
those who are willing to understand
that you must remove yourself far away
from bad with evil
so in peace your soul heart with mind may dwell.

◆ ◆ ◆

NO.39 PACKED

Our planet it is filled to the brim of life of all kinds
birds of the air clothed in beautiful pretty colours
animals large small timid very wild
dangerous deadly man eater's
mouths filled with razor sharpened teeths
alligators with crocodiles.
  Fishes swimming in the deep blue oceans
  also in the moving seas
  as the sailing ships filled up with passengers
  sailing it's constant flowing deep waters
  dolphins sharkes whales octupuses sting rays
  all down there living faraway
  from the lands stable borders.
Busy overcrowded world class cities
filled with tens of millions of people
daily actively on the go hour after hour
cars vans buses coaches pushbikes
moped's motorbikes with lorries.
  Out pops the umbrella's

when the rains start to drop with it's wet shower's
from land to land from country to country
contenant to contenant
separated from the forever flowing blues seas.
Lands covered with hills valley's
cliffs with high mountains
filled with diverse beautiful flowers
clothed in their majestic beauties.

◆ ◆ ◆

NO.40   SHELVES

Just take a stroll down to your local library
go to one of the many shelves collection's
choices you will see you will have confronting you
many a novel in their labelled selection's.
Shelves filled up with story books
for young children of a young early age
there are also shelves for the growing teenager's
more shelves filled with books
for the mature adults of this age.
The library it's there to serve all ages well
keeping you up with these modern ages
internet accesss have been installed in many
I do hope you have your personal library card
they are free to use they don't even cost a penny.
Many authors creating books
many a people who just love to creatively write
books filled with all types of knowledge
taking your dear souls from out of the dark
turning them very bright.

❖ ❖ ❖

NO.41   SHOW

There is some much I have learned from word's
I usually can tell a persons character
just by what they are saying
sensible people uphold wise conversation's
filled with knowledge also sense
you can understand what they are exactly speaking
  The unwise their mouths are filled with foolishness
  many a time when they speak
  their tongue's start inventing lies
  trying to fool people with fibs which are cheap
  but if you are smart also wise
  you will be able to see through their crafty lies
  trying to fool people with fibs which are very cheap.
I have not much time to waste away
listening to imaginary unrealisitc
fables of the pretender's
speaking words without knowledge
when my ears detect it my heart tells my mind
I am listening to another time waster.

❖ ❖ ❖

NO.42   PEOPLE

Just people we are
people daily living out our lives
on this one gigantic planet
men women boy's with girl's
daily living as now become a living habit.
   Young middle aged with old
   all starting out life with a precious dear inner soul
   many of us lose our dear souls in this living life
   long before we reach the ages which are old.
Many don,t mind living their lives soul less
for they know they are not alone
while living in a lost confused puzzled world
which at time can leave you feeling cold and lonely
right down to your bones.

◆ ◆ ◆

NO.43   LOVE

Through word's we learn to express
really how we feel about each other
 kind sweet dear loving word's
pour out from our hearts straight to our lovers.
   Compassionate kind loyal word's
   your two ears will now hear also detect

when your partner is really in love with you
  it,s your heart with mind they do not wish to vex.
Sincere kind even caring
we all need our companions to be
staying honest to us and faithful
staying right by our side not wanting to leave.
  Love should never stand alone
  it should always add up
  multiplying then swiftly spread.

NO.44   READING

He opened up the big thick big book
starting to read one page at a time
Gensis Exodus Leviticus
he continued patiently reading on for a little while.
  Number Joshau Judges Ruth
  his fingers flicked on through.
  while he just started to read through the word's
  in this book filled up with many pages
  which to his eyes were very true
  1st and 2nd samuel 1st and 2nd Kings
  Chronicles one and Chronicles two.
He kept reading through this book
he didn't take his eyes of it
Ezre Nehemiah Esther Job Psalms Proverbs
he didn,t miss a single bit.
  Ecclesiastes the Songs of Soloman
  Isiah Jeremiah
  the words from the holy bible

it was him it always inspired.

NO.45   FICTION

Unreal untrue stories which are fable
childrens books with adventures filled with fantasy's.
imaginary worlds,fairy tales,comical character's
the little boys with girls wishing they were real.
    Books filled with dreamlike stories
    causing your imagination's to run frantic all wild
    a lot of suspense very exciting
    other chapters which are merry
    amicable dainty very mild.
It take's your mind on a mysterious journey
travelling in time on through into peculiar world's
you can get very attached
to some of their interesting charatcter's
right down to your now exicted twitching nerves.
    Some of them becoming just like your friend
    you even wished at times you were just like them
    really wishing they were real people waiting for you
    around that next corner with imaginary bend.

◆ ◆ ◆

NO.46 NON-FICTION

Hardback soft back even e.book digital form
it doesn't really matter what is the cover

I am more interested in what real things
are inside of this book I am going to discover.
   Books of facts truth they do not lack
   books of information's with pages
   filled of instruction's real life stories
   now I'm heading in the right direction.
We all have different taste's
in the books we like to read
some people prefer newspapers
even glossy magazines.
   History books geography books
   chemistry physics with science books
   they all pack up the shelves in the library's
   you will also find them in shops
   inside the shopping malls.
     Religious books spiritual books
     books for healing our souls with minds
     books for physical activities
     cook books for healthy foods with diets
     all in their lines.

◆ ◆ ◆

NO.47   LIKE

What is it you admire
what interests your attentive eye's
is it the word's I am writing
right infront of your reading eye's.
   Please tell me what is it you like
   remember everyone has an hobby
   mine is creative writing

putting pen to paper or tapping away busily
   on my key board with monitor.
Do you like outdoor activities
running bike riding horse trecking
maybe standing by the river side
holding your fishing rod while you are fishing.
   There must be something that you like
   maybe there is something in your life
   which is really missing
   if I were in a position like you my friend
   I would find myself an hobby to be interested in.

◆ ◆ ◆

NO.48   LONG

He took the platform
he started to speak in the long lenghty wide hall
which was filled up with many seats
the crowded room was silenced by the speaker's voice
he had some much things to say
in this large building where you could hear no noise.
   The people were all keen has they sat there
   like they were all in a big team
   listening patiently to this man
   learning to understand the vision's of his dream's.
Very long was his speach in the seminar
he stood there upright amongst the crowd
standing in his position right in the buildings center.
   His aim was to win some souls today
   through the power of his speach
   a learned man a scholar was he

born into this life to help also teach
as he stood there uprightly
sure and confident on his feet.

◆ ◆ ◆

NO.49 INTERESTING

I really really liked it
I am thinking of going back again
it was very fascinating
stimulating my mental brain.
   It wasn't dull neither boring
   no one accidentally feel asleep starting to loudly snore
   it was well worth the while
   when it finished I walked away with a big smile.
I am going back again
this time I am bringing with me a friend
no way am I going to be missing out
I am very serious with no need to pretend.
   It filled me up with charm
   really I was very alarmed
   intrigued while watching
   my mind was filled with calm.

◆ ◆ ◆

NO.50 ENTERTAINING

Her performance was great
she was a very interesting person to watch
causing me to think with wonder
I was in awe astonished and very shocked.
　She is very talented
　just by all the things she could do
　she can easily teach a large multitude
　not just a tiny little few.
Everyone is talented
we all are gifted in one way or another
it,s just are you wise and smart enough
to find your inner treasure's.
　We all like to be entertained
　blesssed though are the entertainers
　for when they appear arrive and finally come
　they are always filled with life's amazing saving
　flavour's of fun.

◆ ◆ ◆

NO.51　　WORTH

How much are you valued by people
is your respect very high or graded low

by the way people treat you
your own common-senses will silently let you know.
    How much are people worth to you
    are they appreciated in your eye's
    will you go that extra mile for them
    for they are really worth your ticking time.
A genuine good close friend
you will find very worthy indeed
for they will know when you need their support
when you really need them on your team.
    Those people who are worthy
    they don,t want unworthy unreliable friend's
    they wish for honest people like themselves
    to be right by their side
    to protect also to properly defend.

◆ ◆ ◆

NO.52   LOOK

I started to take note while noticing
just by the way each individual spoke
I would pay close attention
to the words which came up from out of their throat.
    I spotted her from a distance away
    this young lady she is looking very fine
    when she spoke her voice was very calming
    I could not help myself
    I stayed listening to her for quite some time.
After leaving her pleasant side
I found myself walking all alone for a little while
until I noticed from a distance

spotting another stranger through my eager eye's.
   An old fella sitting on a park bench
   I started to walk right near by
   as I was about to pass him
  we both caught each others eye
   I noticed a large gap in his mouth
   where his four front teeth use to be
   as he smiled then started to grin at me.

NO.53   SPEND

You could easily tell what her hobby was
whenever you entered her family home
this young girl spent most of her time in her bedroom
feeling comfortably with herself being all alone.
   She had her own book shelf
   fixed securely to her bedroom wall
   the shelf was completely filled with books
   all placed next to one another very neatly
   she looked after everyone of them very well.
She was a lover of story books
there she laid right now on her bed
a book opened up wide in her hand
as she looked down at it and silently read.
   It's good to spend a little time on your own
   it doesn't matter the age you are
   a little silent reading can take your mind away
   to pleasant pleasing places away very far.

NO.54　　LITTLE

At his hospital bed side
his parents stood right beside him looking very worried
their young son had been in a terrible accident
so they both together rushed to his bedside
hours ago in a frantic hurry.
　He had suffered head injurie's
　laying there in a coma deeply unconscious
　inside of the hospital bed
　his dad held on tightly to his mother
　between them tiers rolled down the faces
　as very little was being said.
A hospital drip was attached to the boy's hand
while a digital machine
constantly monitored his heart beats
as a doctor dressed all in white
was standing right next to this little boy
testing his temperature
concerned about this young boy,s body heat.
　All who were around his bed side seem very worried
　the doctors facial expressions did not look pleased
　you could feel the tension in the hospital wards room
　if you were there you would be wishing
　it would quickly ease.
All of a sudden the little boy
quickly opened up both his eye's
his parent's with the doctor were amazed with shock
the boy then said just a few little word's
the doctor was now relieved
for he knew life the little boy still had got.

NO.55 MONEY

It,s money that makes our material world go around
it keep's the rich with poor people all busy on their feet
the whole entire world is after it
the more you achieve it's the further away
you are moved from ugly defeat.
   Young with old,high class and low class
    everyone wishes for a load of it
    inside of their bank accounts
    the genuine people with the robbers
    even the crooked thieves
    also the rogue with vagrant beggar with the tramp.
Pennies pounds hundreds lovely thousand's
this is still little and not large amounts
the wise with the intelligent clever and smart
they are seeking for hundreds of thousand's
inside of their bank accounts
I am sorry it,s million's infact.
    One million two million and more
    this will appear into their lives
    all of those people who are honest very sure
    will be bringing satisfaction
    so then no more will they have a need to strive.

NO.56 BUY

The word's of wisdom they are not for sale
it's something you just can't buy
for this is one thing in this worldly life
which is free for you even I.
    The poor wise man was full of knowledge
    he knew the answers to many things
    one day in time he was gathered away
    being brought by wise counsellor's
    to the mighty ruling reigning king.
You could see concern covered the ruler's face
worries could be seen noticed easily spotted
his own wise men of his rich and wealthy province
could not help him with his problem
he had received also had gotten.
    The king had been for a lenght of time restless
    being robbed of his night sleep for endless nights
    for every time he closed his eyes ready for slumber
    all his dreams were filled with terrors
    horrors gruesome dreadful aweful frights.
All his wise men had no real explanation's
they just couldn,t transulate their ruler's dreams
which rose up great anger in the king of the land
he started treating all his servants with noblemen
cruel and very mean.
The poor wise man stood
now infront of the great ruler
already knowing the answer's
to the ruler's crazy weird strange mysterious dreams.

NO.57   SOMETHING

She had been searching for quite some time
she also knew herself one day
she would eventually find
the only problem was how long and when ?
the answer she didn,t know in her mind.
    He also was on the seek and find
    while his lonely heart was always aching
    looking for a dear lady
    so she may share her days of life with him.
It seems everyone is on the search and seek
we all are after something
sometime we just don,t know what it is
but we do know something very important is missing.
    I am daily on the search
    all over the face of this precious earth
    searching until one day I will find
    finding whatever in my life is really missing.

◆ ◆ ◆

NO.58 YOU MAKE ME

You make me think and start to wonder by your action's
 also by the strange way you speak very loud
very intimidating and aggressive

cursing and swearing everyday.
   You are always clothing yourself in violence
    while thinking you are tough hard and smart
    your ego is in over-drive
   while you puff out your chest grin smerk then laugh.
Out of steel you think you have been created
when in reality it's just simply flesh with bone's
the hospital wards are filled up
overflowing with violent brutish brutal people
like a routine
it is becoming some of their second home's.

◆ ◆ ◆

NO.59 THROW AWAY

You really don,t need it
I see it spoils your image straight away
vulgar speach with bad language
while you walk rock also sway.
   You have that natural beauty
  most men find your feminine feature's
   attractive straight away
  but you are dis-appointing your ownself
 as soon as you open up your mouth to speak then say.
Well dressed up in his expensive looking suit
he is the best man on this wedding day
he gulped down way to much strong drink this evening
then acted the big red nose circus clown
spoiling his best friends special day.
   She went into her kitchen
    leaving her purse on the living rooms coffee table

quite a few money note were inside
   her so-called best friend opened it up
   taking out a twenty pound note on the sly.
Come on people throw away
now your dirty bad habit's
the crooked ways which are shifty
crude vulgar even vile.

NO.60 HAVE

Fortunate people we are
for we have the ability of reason
it,s because the blessed words dwell with us
in every single moving season.
   Different are we as human's
   to all the other creature's in this land
   we are separated from all other species
   for precious words for speach we always have at hand.
We have the understanding
to properly eastablish and to build
we as humans have the power
we have all the resources with the will.
   To rule to lead to guide
   too protect to shelter to safely deliver
   anything we put our human minds too
  we can achieve for we are blessed with earthly power's.

NO.61   REACHING

We learn as we grow
many of us are reaching out
seeking for answers with meanings
to what this living life is all about.
　Some may not be interested
　some may not be intrigued
　I certainly am very fascinated
　why I am created to live a life as a human being.
If you are eager in searching
for life it,s curious answer's
please keep reaching out with no intention's
to withdraw yourself neither surrender.
　Those people who have ambitous goal's
　they are reaching out all of the time
　they all are desiring to achieve rewards
　all splendid things which to them are divine.

◆ ◆ ◆

NO.62 END

I have stated already
I will say it again
the word's of wisdom they are eternal
lasting forever and ever my reading friend's.

The simple word which pops out from our mouths
  every time we start to speak
  it,s not a shallow thing in this world
  it is powerful also very deep.
For by the word's of world leader's
wars can start or wars can cease
a person can be enslaved by a word
even freely freed being totally set free.
  They can be brought to high honour
  praised by many in high position's
  the word setting them up high in society
  the word's to you may seem invaluable
   to all those who are wise they are precious and mighty.

◆ ◆ ◆

NO.63   DO NOT

I know we all are learning
I have certainly learnt a lot
now I will give you a little advice
from the information I have received also gladly got.
  Don,t stop seeking for knowledge
  until it fills up your precious souls
  it will set a comfortable flame burning bright in you
  keeping the passion you have from growing cold.
Don,t fret neither worry yourself
I know your future it,s going to be
much more finer than your past
for wisdom knowledge with understanding
you have diligently store up inside of your heart.
  Do not under-estimate the power's of holy wisdom

your search for it will not end up in vain
you were wise enough to find it
so now its all just a matter of time
before you greatly gain.

◆ ◆ ◆

NO.64   WILL

I am out here trying
It does not mean though I will succeed
well not straight away
it may take a little while indeed.
  I will not stop trying though
  until every single thing properly connect's
  when all perfect lines come together
  I will then be on a brandnew stage
  which we call the next.
From poverty to riches
from foolish speach to intelligent talk
we all have to creep a little
before we strongly stand
getting up to now steadily walk.
  So don't come off your chosen honest path
  we already know is genuine and true
  you have the installed will power inside of you
  so please continue on to pursue.

◆ ◆ ◆

NO.65　　PROBABLY

I didn,t think it was an accident
it was probably just a silly error
it could of been a simple mistake
nothing though man makes remember is perfect.
　　Machines do slow down at times
　　they can even operate way to late
　　there is always a probability
　　that things can go awefully wrong
　　everything that man does make
　　doesn,t stay forever strong.
Mankind they are very good at creating
you can see the world is filled with their invention's
it is also filled with manmade catastrophies
including a lot of manmade desaster's.
　　The men of the world are always attempting
　　 probably they will never ever stop
　　for their hearts are filled up with so many
　　creative imaginations
　　they are forever inventing creative creation's
　　right around the twenty four hour time clock.

◆ ◆ ◆

NO.66　　HAND

So wise is our creator
H.E know's exactlywhat we need
H.E made sure *H.E* created hands for us
so we can pick up things also touch even feel.
   We can open up a book
   so we may start to read
   hold our spoons knives with fork's
   so our ownselves we can daily feed.
We can wash ourselves all over
before putting on our clothes
pick up some after-shave or maybe purfume
giving it a little sniff with our nose.
   We can close both our hands
   clenching tight our fists ready for a fight
   we can place our palms together
   prepared now to say our prays late at night.
Our hands they are very versatile
without them there is not much in life we can do
we would be completely lost without our hands
it is a no win situation
for greatly without our hands
in life we would surely lose.

◆ ◆ ◆

NO.67   ONE

Just one single word
can make a big change
one word I am telling you can keep you calm
or send you flying into a rage.
   Just one single word I am telling you

        don't even seem very surprised
        why should I lie to you
        the truth I will not deny.
One percific wrong word
can turn your friend into your enemy
it can call troops with regiments of soldier's off to battle
forming a great fighting army against you also me.
        So please be careful with your speach
        select sensible the word's of your mouth
        remember your own voice
        can get you in deep dangerous trouble's
        if you always allow it to carelessly
        freely roam all about.

◆ ◆ ◆

NO.68   FRIEND'S

Beautiful kind word's
bringing people together
creating among the fellow people good friends
all sharing interests with good topics with one another.
        Sharping each other with word's again and again
        knowledge shared with each other
        only makes us become more brighter also wiser
        you shall be feeling fine
        while the finer get more finer even finer.
You can even turn your enemy into your friend
showing them exactly where the both of you
seem to of being going wrong.
good honest words fix seal they strongly fasten
clearing away the bitter atmosphere

so in peace we may continue also prolong.
    It's really great to have good friend's
    securely fixed by your side
    true friend's with honest friend's
    who will share life with you to the uttermost end.

◆ ◆ ◆

NO.69   MORE

We are learning all of the time
learning more and more and more
knowledge it is certainly increasing
as earthly worldly time is steadily on the roll.
  The more you learn
   it's the deeper your inner thoughts develope and grow
   strenghtening your mental balance
  so you may stay positively confident for sure.
So keep on buying books of knowledge
you will continue then to learn much more
it is healthy and very good for your dear hungry souls
to take good information in through your mental doors.
    There is no end to knowledge
    on our planet it is increasing all of the time
    from the days of old the ancient generation's
    from the earliest human civilization's
    those remembered days now all behind.
Each generation learning from the last
the present age always evolving from the past
progressive progression progressing positively
so then prosperity may manifest
showing all we are enduring

while growing wiser in our human hearts.

◆ ◆ ◆

NO.70 READ

We have finally arrived at the last page of this book
I really do hope that you enjoyed the read
do not give up on reading books
for it,s something very important your mind needs.
  I have a lot more books of knowledge out there
  covering a range of all different types of topics
  I do hope when you find the time with moment
  you can buy for yourself a brand-new different copy.
They will all be out there on the book shop shelves
more than forty five other different types with kinds
let me see if you are smart enough
to seek out for more of my books to gladly find.
   keep on reading taking information in
   for it shall certainly broaden your thinking minds
   making you wise just like a king.
   read the word's but please do understand them
   take note while you read on through every line.

◆ ◆ ◆

nathaniel.s.bird